A season of sundays

Images of the 2013 Gaelic Games year by the Sportsfile team of photographers, with text by Alan Milton

An official GAA publication, published by Sportsfile

Supporting GAA for 23 years

Carroll's is once again delighted to be a sponsor of *A Season of Sundays,* Sportsfile's celebrated pictorial review of the football and hurling seasons.

Our sponsorship of the book is an extension of the company's involvement in Gaelic games as we have been proud to sponsor the Offaly county teams for the past 23 years, enjoying many memorable days along the way.

In 1991, when the GAA first allowed sponsorship of county shirts, Carroll's (then Carroll's Meats) was the first name on the Offaly shirt and it has remained there ever since, making it the longest running sponsorship in the GAA.

2013 was another terrific year, culminating in two outstanding teams, Dublin and Clare, winning the All-Ireland senior football and hurling titles.

However, 2013 was also a busy year at Carroll's. Besides extending our sponsorship of the Offaly teams, we set a unique world record for making the greatest number of ham sandwiches, and in the process we raised much needed funds and awareness for Irish Autism Action.

The record was achieved on Sunday 9th June, before the Offaly-Kilkenny Leinster hurling clash, when 50 volunteers made 3,145 Carroll's ham sandwiches in 37 minutes at Tullamore GAA club.

We also fielded a new range of exciting ham flavours with our Carroll's handcrafted range and we were prominent at both the Tullamore Show and the National Ploughing Championships, where thousands of people enjoyed our products.

Carroll's is fully committed to giving back to our Irish heritage and the company's continued support of Gaelic games and *A Season of Sundays* is part of that commitment.

From Dingle to Donegal, from Derry to Dungarvan, we hope you enjoyed many a Carroll's ham sandwich on the way to Croke Park this year – and that you will continue to do so in 2014.

The Carroll's Team

sportsfile
PUBLISHING

GAA
OFFICIAL PHOTOGRAPHER

Published by:
SPORTSFILE
Patterson House, 14 South Circular Road
Portobello, Dublin 8, Ireland
www.sportsfile.com

Photographs:
Copyright © 2013 Sportsfile

ISBN: 978-1-905468-25-6

Text:
Alan Milton

Editing:
Eddie Longworth

Quotations research:
Seán Creedon

Additional photographs:
Ray Ryan

Design:
The Design Gang, Tralee

Colour reproduction:
Mark McGrath

Print production:
Paul Bolger, PB Print Solutions

Printing:
Hudson Killeen Ltd, Dublin

Case Binding:
Robinson & Mornin Bookbinders Ltd, Belfast

The Sportsfile photographic team:

Barry Cregg

Brian Lawless

Brendan Moran

Dáire Brennan

David Maher

Diarmuid Greene

Matt Browne

Oliver McVeigh

Pat Murphy

Paul Mohan

Ray McManus

Stephen McCarthy

In the right place at the right time

Being in the right place at the right time has always been my aim as a photographer. I have been privileged to be in that position many times in 2013, but two occasions particularly stand out.

The first was at Nowlan Park on Saturday July 6 for the hurling qualifier between Kilkenny and Tipperary. With six minutes to go and Kilkenny struggling to kill off Tipp's challenge, manager Brian Cody calls on Henry Shefflin, who had missed the Cats' three earlier championship games through injury.

I can vividly recall that moment – Cody was on the line and I was standing between Shefflin and the wall. Not only did I photograph Shefflin's entrance but I heard Cody's last words of advice to him.

The instruction to one of the greatest hurlers of all time from one of the greatest managers of all time was simply "Just go out and play". There were no clipboards or indecipherable hand gestures that we see in so many other sports, just a simple remark between two great men who trust each other.

The other occasion that sticks out is being in the Dublin dressingroom after they had won the Leinster hurling title for the first time since 1961. Normally – and understandably – access is limited to dressingrooms but Dublin manager Anthony Daly invited me to be present. The celebrations were boisterous to say the least, and yet the noise immediately subsided when the Galway manager Anthony Cunningham entered to congratulate Dublin. There were calls for ciúnas, silence descended and respect was shown to the losing manager.

It's witnessing events such as these that makes the job of a sports photographer so enjoyable and fulfilling. It was a terrific season but what made it even more memorable for me was seeing my native county, Dublin, enjoy significant success, with the hurlers winning the Leinster title and the footballers lifting the Sam Maguire Cup – and doing so with a vibrant, attacking style of play.

The Liam MacCarthy Cup was also won by an outstanding team. Clare's young side brought hurling to a new level with their sublime skills and sophisticated game plan.

Each year I'm impressed by the professionalism of our team here in the Sportsfile agency as they set out to capture that exceptional picture, something above the ordinary. They operate in all kinds of weather and their commitment and attention to detail are vital to this project. We hope you enjoy the fruits of their labour.

Finally, a special word of thanks to Carroll's, the sponsors of this publication. The Carroll's company has deep roots in the GAA and their financial backing of the Offaly football and hurling teams is the longest running sponsorship in the association.

Ray McManus

Scoth Bliana

Is cúis mhór áthais dom an deis seo a bheith agam na focail seo a leanas a scríobh don leabhar iontach seo.

Every now and then there comes a season that reinvigorates us and reminds us all why we are so passionate about our games.

A season – or in this case a year – that captivates and bewilders, entertains and mystifies, enthrals and crucially leaves us yearning for more. 2013 was one such year.

The embers of the action are still warm and the afterglow still detectable - especially in the counties of Clare and Dublin - but the past year was about so much more than winning teams.

It didn't start with the championship either. Dublin's footballers once again used Croke Park as the launch pad for what would turn out to be a memorable seven-month period of activity during which they lost only one competitive game. It was a run that allowed Dublin to claim a first National Football League title since 1993 and, in the process, send out a signal of intent.

In hurling, The National League final between Kilkenny and Tipperary was played in Nowlan Park in something of a dry run for a memorable mid-summer encounter between the same teams at the same venue. Kilkenny won both games and yet neither of these traditional powers won a championship title.

On St Patrick's Day, victories for St Thomas' and St Brigid's meant that the All-Ireland club championship titles went to Connacht. St Thomas' beat Kilcormac Killoughey in the hurling final and St Brigid's edged out Ballymun Kickhams in football.

If the football championship remained constant in the way it unfolded, with many of the top teams of recent seasons still to the fore, the hurling version did not go along familiar lines.

We all have our own highlights. Was it Monaghan's breakthrough success in Ulster or the hurling breakthroughs for Limerick and Dublin in Munster and Leinster that made you sit up and take notice?

Or Clare's emergence as one of the youngest All-Ireland challenging teams since Cork's team of 1999? Or perhaps it was something less obvious. It could have been Antrim hurlers' All-Ireland under-21 semi-final success over Wexford, Carlow's under-21 Leinster hurling win over Dublin or Waterford's emergence in the minor hurling championship.

As ever our finals were memorable occasions, days that make a connection with Irish people everywhere. They didn't disappoint this year and incredibly, following last year's draw between Kilkenny and Galway, the need for another hurling final replay arose.

Was there anything, anywhere, that offered the standard of entertainment we were treated to in the two hurling finals between Clare and Cork or in the closing stages of the football championship? At the end of it all, Dublin lifted the Sam Maguire Cup and the Liam MacCarthy Cup went to Clare.

Crucially Ray McManus and his team were present to capture all the big matches and so much more besides.

While the results quite often generate the headlines they are a product of so many incidents, twists and turns and factors that would go unnoticed and unrecorded were it not for the shutters of the Sportsfile cameras. Every corner of Ireland – with the occasional venue further afield – features, as do so many of the players who illuminate our games and our championships.

Crucially what features between these two covers serves as a record for the past 12 months, one that finds a place in so many homes. You only have to take out old editions of the book to see how it stands the test of time. The jerseys, fashions and hairstyles may change but the high stakes and the interest the games arouse remain the same.

To that end we owe Ray and his team of talented photographers a debt of gratitude. Their attention to detail, professionalism and passion for our games underpin the success of this publication, now in its 17th year.

Where else would you see so many of our volunteers standing shoulder to shoulder with the top names in our games? And is there any other such vehicle that caters for this year-in, year-out?

Where else would you get the images you expect from our biggest events but crucially those you don't expect from lesser celebrated gatherings?

I'm looking forward to charting the season that was 2013 and I hope you are too.

Bainigí sult as.

Liam Ó Néill

Liam Ó Néill
Uachtarán Cumann Lúthchleas Gael

6 Bord na Móna O'Byrne Cup - Kilanerin Ballyfad GAA Club, Co. Wexford
Wexford 1-11   DIT 1-15

Bord na Móna O'Byrne Cup - County Grounds, Drogheda
Louth 2-15   UCD 1-13

1.

(1) The ink barely dry. The improvised scoreboard at the Kilanerin Ballyfad club before the early-season meeting of hosts Wexford and Dublin Institute of Technology

(2) Tús maith leath na hoibre. Michael Coyle takes stock of the situation and prepares the 'crockery'

6   Connacht FBD League - Elphin GAA Club, Co. Roscommon
Roscommon 0-05   Leitrim 0-06

Power NI Dr. McKenna Cup - Healy Park, Omagh
Tyrone 1-14   Derry 0-15

McGrath Cup - St Joseph's Miltown Malbay GAA Club, Co. Clare
Clare 1-20   LIT 1-02

1.

" You can only play what's in front of you, but our fellows played good attractive football today. They combined well, but there is a lot of work to be done yet **"**
Clare manager Mick O'Dwyer gets off to a good start as the Banner are easy winners over Limerick IT in the McGrath Cup

(1) Entrez. Gothic or Romanesque? The Connacht football league takes John Evans and Roscommon off the beaten track

(2) Running a different line. Cavan's Maggie Farrelly makes history by becoming the first female intercounty match official

(3) The Evangelist. Mick O'Dywer's latest port of call on the management circuit takes him to Cusack Park, Ennis. The usual buzz accompanies his arrival

6 Bord na Móna O'Byrne Cup - Ballymahon GAA club, Co. Longford
Longford 1-07   Meath 1-09

Bord na Móna O'Byrne Cup - O'Connor Park, Tullamore
Offaly 1-11   Laois 1-08

2.

(1) Meet you halfway. Managers Glenn Ryan and Mick O'Dowd
exchange pleasantries in the humble surroundings of
Ballymahon's sideline

(2) One for all and all for one. Offaly football manager Emmet
McDonnell stands to attention alongside his charges as his
pride restoration project begins

9 Bord na Móna O'Byrne Cup - Emmet Park, Killoe, Co. Longford
Longford 1-14   UCD 0-14

Power NI Dr. McKenna Cup - Brewster Park, Enniskillen
Fermanagh 2-15   Donegal 2-07

(1) Not quite a flood of lights but action nonetheless as Longford host UCD at Killoe

(2) Sonar or radar? Heavy fog envelopes Enniskillen for the meeting of Donegal and Fermanagh

1.

2.

1.

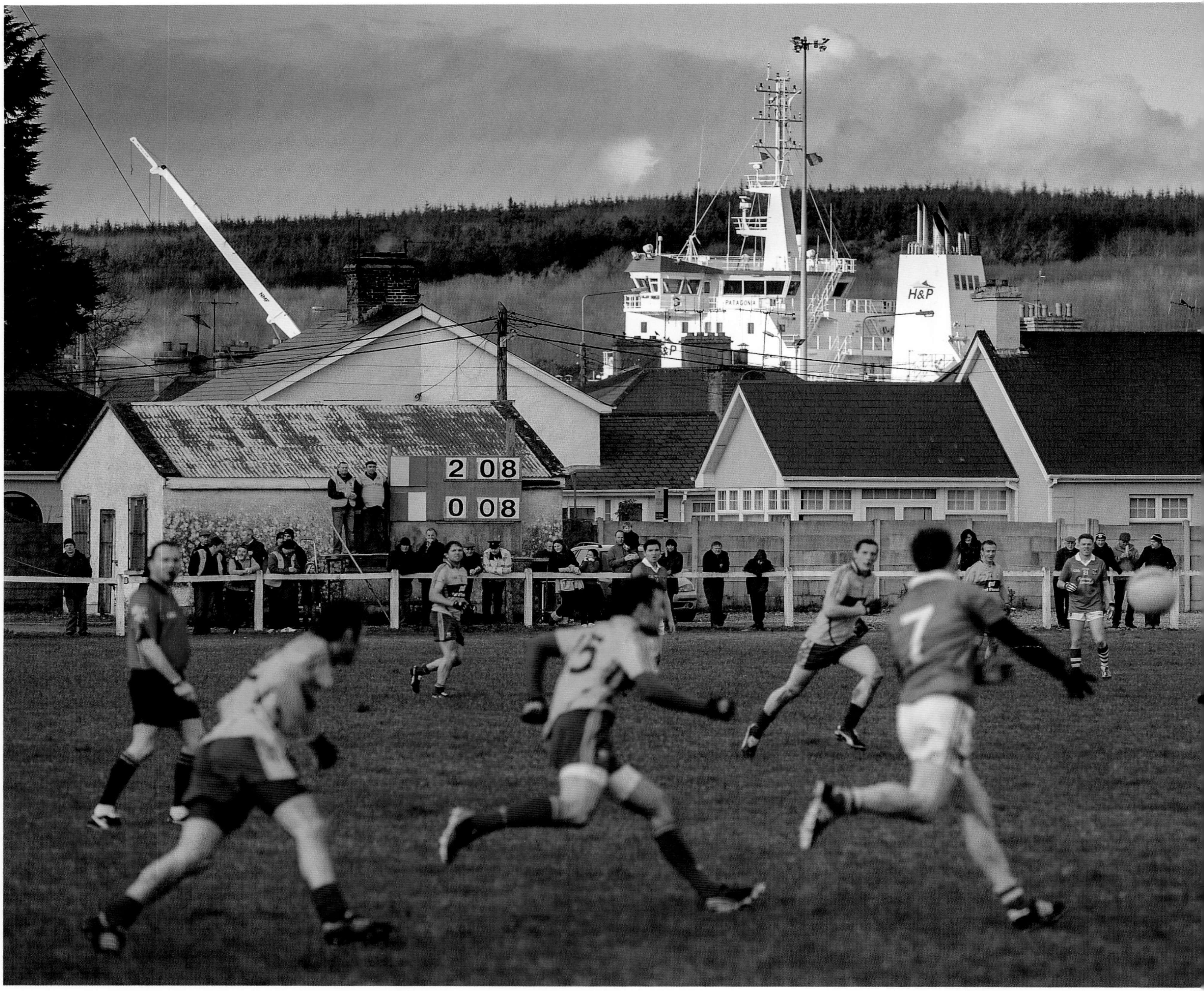

13

McGrath Cup - Páirc na nGael, Foynes, Co. Limerick
Limerick 2-16   Clare 2-13

McGrath Cup - Páirc Uí Rinn, Cork
Cork 1-09   Tipperary 2-09

Bord na Móna O'Byrne Cup - Cusack Park, Mullingar
Westmeath 0-07   Offaly 0-08

Power NI Dr. McKenna Cup - Casement Park, Belfast
Antrim 1-10   Tyrone 2-13

2.

3.

4.

(1) Full steam ahead. Clare and Limerick do battle in Foynes under the watchful eye of a locally docked vessel

(2) 'It was this big!' Eoin Cadogan chats with team-mates Noel O'Leary and Michael Shields before the second half. Perhaps Cork were too laid-back as Tipperary recorded their first win over the Rebels since 1944

(3) Taste of leather – almost. Alan McNamee goes low and hard against Denis Corroon of Westmeath

(4) Brace yourself. Colm Fleming attempts to thwart a Mattie Donnelly strike for Tyrone

13 Bord na Móna O'Byrne Cup - St. Conleth's Park, Newbridge
Kildare 1-13 Wexford 1-11

Connacht FBD League - Páirc Seán O'Heslin, Ballinamore
Leitrim 0-09 Mayo 0-08

(1) Multi-layered. Well prepared for the cold, Jason Ryan and Kieran McGeeney follow the play

(2) Strike a pose. Emlyn Mulligan's gait and the gaze of the players follow what will turn out to be a Leitrim winner against Mayo in Ballinamore

1.

2.

20 Connacht FBD League - Enniscrone Kilglass GAA Club, Co. Sligo
Sligo 0-09 Galway 1-04

Bord na Móna O'Byrne Cup - County Grounds, Drogheda
Louth 0-10 Dublin 4-15

Power NI Dr. McKenna Cup - Athletic Grounds, Armagh
Monaghan 1-12 Down 0-13

1.

3.

(1) A multi-purpose building. The facilities at Enniscrone Kilglass hold the scoreboard and flags, provide a stretching area for referee Frank Flynn and serve as a vantage point for videographers

(2) One fist useful, two hands better. Tyrone native Paddy Quinn gathers possession for Dublin against Adrian Reid of Louth

(3) Shoulder-shielding. Monaghan's Darren Hughes goes low to evade the probing hand of Ryan Mallon of Down

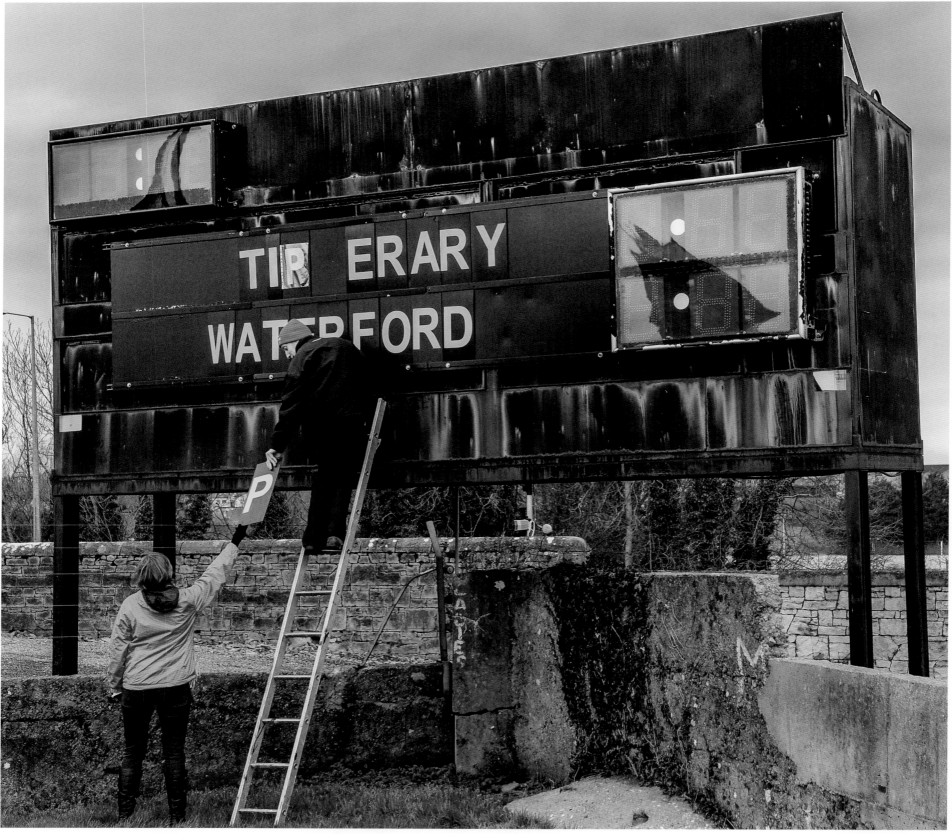

2.

(1) Two Ps in a pod. Claire O'Brien and Francis Coughlan mix and match to replace the missing letter before Tipperary's meeting with Waterford at Seán Treacy Park

(2) A white haze. UTV camera man John Vernard braves the elements on the gantry for Tyrone's meeting with Fermanagh

26 Power NI Dr. McKenna Cup Final - Athletic Grounds, Armagh
Tyrone 4-11   Monaghan 1-10

McGrath Cup Final - Seán Treacy Park, Tipperary
Kerry 1-12   Tipperary 1-05

Bord na Móna O'Byrne Cup Final - Parnell Park, Dublin
Dublin 0-17   Kildare 1-16

1.

2.

3.

(1) Forget the ribbons. Although blue and white adorns the Dr McKenna Cup the night belongs to Stephen O'Neill and Tyrone who see off the challenge of Monaghan

(2) Tournament victories and reserved celebrations. Kerry captain Anthony Maher does the honours and his attire confirms the victory has been won on soft fields

(3) Kildare captain Mikey Conway lifts the O'Byrne Cup after a final success over Dublin. A sign of things to come?

(4) Respect. The Dublin footballers honour the memory of Kevin Heffernan who did more to popularise the famed sky-blue shirt than anyone

2.

(1) Marooned. Séamus Moore from Carlow town cuts a solitary figure as he removes the Galway colours after the visitors had beaten the host county

(2) No red carpet. Tipperary hurlers make their way to the pitch for the second half watched by supporters Tom Grace, David Enright and 14-year-old Ciarán Enright

1.

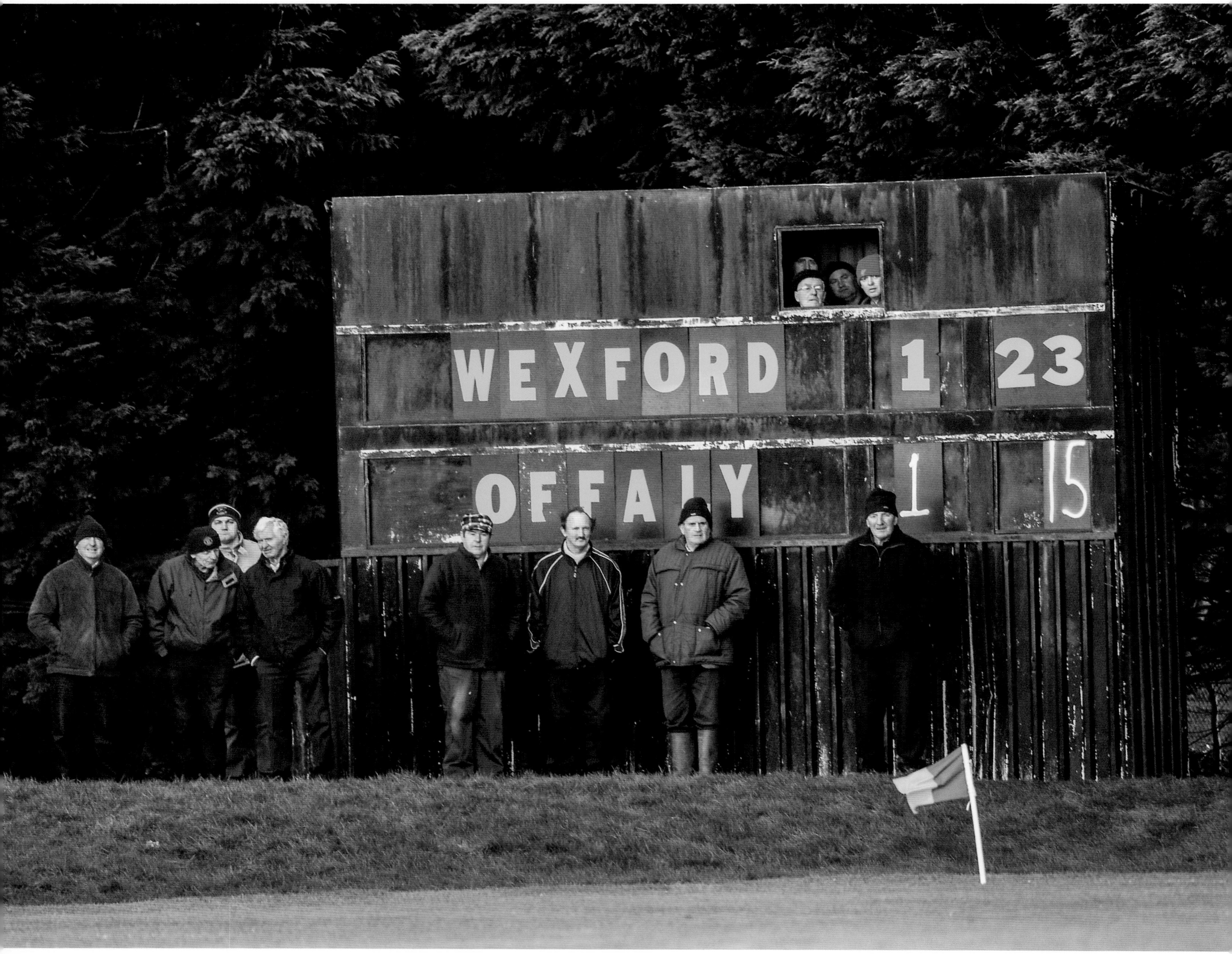

27 Bord na Móna Walsh Cup - Páirc Naomh Bríd, Blackwater GAA Club, Co. Wexford
Wexford 1-24 Offaly 1-15

Connacht FBD League Home Final - Markievicz Park, Sligo
Sligo 0-05 Leitrim 0-08

2.

❝ I think we have turned a corner in the sense that the fear of winning is now no longer there. I have often seen Leitrim teams in the past, when they would have been two or three points up, and would think they weren't entitled to be ahead and they would end up losing **❞**
Leitrim's joint manager Barney Breen after the county's win over Sligo in the FBD League final, their first title success in the competition

(1) No room at the inn. It's a case of a full house at the scoreboard vantage point as Wexford beat Offaly at the Blackwater club

(2) January smiles. Leitrim record a rare title success – the FBD League – at the start of what will be a challenging season

2   Allianz GAA Football National League - Páirc Esler, Newry
Down 1-08   Tyrone 1-11

Allianz GAA Football National League - Croke Park, Dublin
Kildare 2-14   Donegal 1-13

Allianz GAA Football National League - O'Moore Park, Portlaoise
Laois 0-20   Armagh 1-10

Allianz GAA Football National League - Croke Park, Dublin
Dublin 1-18   Cork 2-09

3.

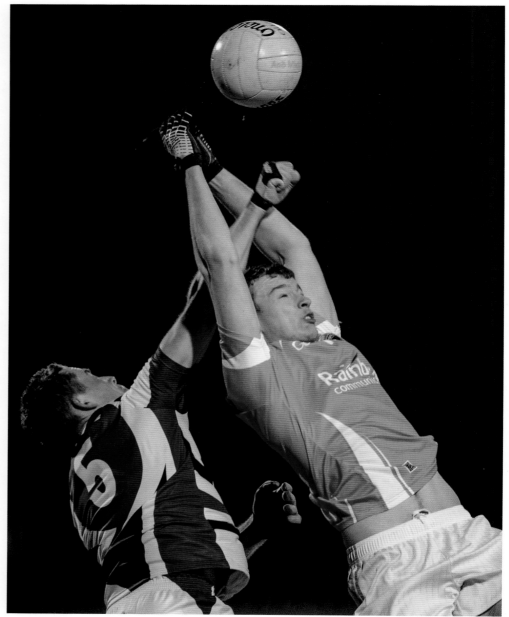

1.

2.

(1) Stairway from heaven? The Down players descend for the league match against Tyrone at Páirc Esler before coming up short

(2) The lure of the big house never seems to recede. Referee Cormac Reilly and his officials pose for a photo at Croke Park

(3) Fumbling in the dark? Ethan Rafferty and Darren Strong get in a tangle without knowing exactly where the ball is

(4) Six feet but only one foot on the ground. Linesman Maurice Deegan maintains some contact with Mother Earth as Michael Darragh Macauley shows perfect balance in attempting to evade Andrew O'Sullivan's challenge

4

" I had a good think about it and Jim (Gavin) assured me of my role so I was happy enough to take it on board and hopefully I'll do the job that he requested "

Dublin goalkeeper Stephen Cluxton talks to the media after his first game as Dublin captain, against Cork in the National League

3 Allianz GAA Football National League - St Tiernach's Park, Clones
Monaghan 1-18   Meath 2-03

Allianz GAA Football National League - Pearse Stadium, Salthill
Galway 1-15   Derry 0-15

2.

(1) Tayto sandwich. Monaghan duo Kieran Hughes and Conor McManus are caught between Meath's Donal Keoghan and Bryan Menton

(2) Not throwing in the towel. Galway's efforts won't be hampered by damp shorts as a result of a wet photo bench. Gerry Moylette from the city goes the extra mile, and his attention to detail pays off as Galway claim the points against Armagh

3 Allianz GAA Football National League - Cusack Park, Mullingar
Westmeath 0-16   Louth 2-09

Allianz GAA Football National League - Wexford Park, Wexford
Wexford 2-08   Longford 1-10

Allianz GAA Football National League - Elverys MacHale Park, Castlebar
Mayo 0-15   Kerry 1-06

Bord na Móna Walsh Cup - Páirc Naomh Bríd, Blackwater GAA Club, Co. Wexford
Wexford 2-18   Kilkenny 0-16

2.

3.

4.

(1) Frozen in time. Louth's David Reid drops the size five on to the size 10 as Ronan Foley of Westmeath lunges

(2) Closing in. The Wexford trio of Redmond Barry, Craig Doyle and Aindreas Doyle have Brendan McElvaney of Longford in their sights

(3) Turning a blind eye? Michael Conroy clutches the ball as Shane Enright gets to grips with him in a Mayo home win over Kerry

(4) Always at each other's throats. PJ Nolan has his windpipe checked by Brian Kennedy, as neighbours Wexford and Kilkenny renew rivalries

9 Waterford Crystal Cup Final - Semple Stadium, Thurles
Clare 1-21   Tipperary 1-13

AIB GAA Hurling All-Ireland Senior Club Championship Semi-Final - O'Moore Park, Portlaoise
Kilcormac Killoughey 1-20   Thurles Sarsfields 1-14

AIB GAA Hurling All-Ireland Senior Club Championship Semi-Final - Parnell Park, Dublin
St Thomas' 1-25   Loughgiel Shamrocks 3-19

1.

2.

(1) Crystal by name and by nature. Clare captain Patrick Donnellan gets in some early practice. He couldn't have known then… could he?

(2) Easy does it. Danny Owens, the Kilcormac Killoughey manager, braces himself for the congratulations of his son John. The Offaly and Leinster champions are Croke Park bound after beating a fancied Thurles Sarsfields

(3) Ground hurling. Loughgiel and St Thomas' serve up a classic on a soft pasture at Parnell Park. Not even extra time can separate them

" We'll savour the night and enjoy it, but by the middle of the week we'll be back to brass tacks **"**

Kilcormac Killoughey manager Danny Owens is keeping a lid on the celebrating after his club's shock win over Thurles Sarsfields in the All-Ireland club hurling semi-final in Portlaoise

3.

10 Allianz GAA Football National League - Pearse Park, Longford
Longford 1-08   Westmeath 2-07

Allianz GAA Football National League - Fitzgerald Stadium, Killarney
Kerry 0-04   Dublin 1-11

1.

2.

(1) A soft day. Spectators have the cover of the stand and photographers use an umbrella
but there is no shelter for the Westmeath players before a league win over Longford

(2) Signal of intent. A one-sided scoreline not often seen in Killarney puts a pep in blue
steps and leaves Kerry with plenty to ponder

16 AIB GAA Football All-Ireland Senior Club Championship Semi-Final - Semple Stadium, Thurles
Ballymun Kickhams 1-10   Dr Crokes 0-09

AIB GAA Football All-Ireland Senior Club Championship Semi-Final - Cusack Park, Mullingar
St Brigid's 2-07   Crossmaglen Rangers 1-09

" I said to them before we went out, if we can put away these greatest of champions there is no question about you boys. Okay they may ask about your medals, but in terms of character, no "

St Brigid's manager Kevin McStay after the Roscommon club ended Crossmaglen's hopes of a three-in-a-row in the club championship

1.

3.

(1) 'The 'Mun, the 'Mun, c'mon the Ballymun!' Braveheart-style paint markings confirm this fan's allegiances in Thurles where Ballymun Kickhams see off Dr Crokes in the semi-final

(2) The smile says it all, never mind the jig. Cake, aka Shane Curran, celebrates his team's second goal in St Brigid's semi-final win over Crossmaglen Rangers

(3) Hot stuff. Ballymun goalkeeper Seán Currie goes low and straight to keep out Chris Brady's penalty under the gaze of a watchful umpire

FEBRUARY '13

17 M. Donnelly GAA Hurling Interprovincial Championship Semi-Final - O'Connor Park, Tullamore
Leinster 1-16   Connacht 3-13

23 Allianz GAA Hurling National League - Parnell Park, Dublin
Dublin 1-20   Offaly 2-16

2.

(1) Chasing shadows. Cyril Donnellan shapes to strike in Connacht's interprovincial win against Leinster in Tullamore

(2) Offloading left. Offaly's David King gets the sliotar away as Danny Sutcliffe sets up a road block

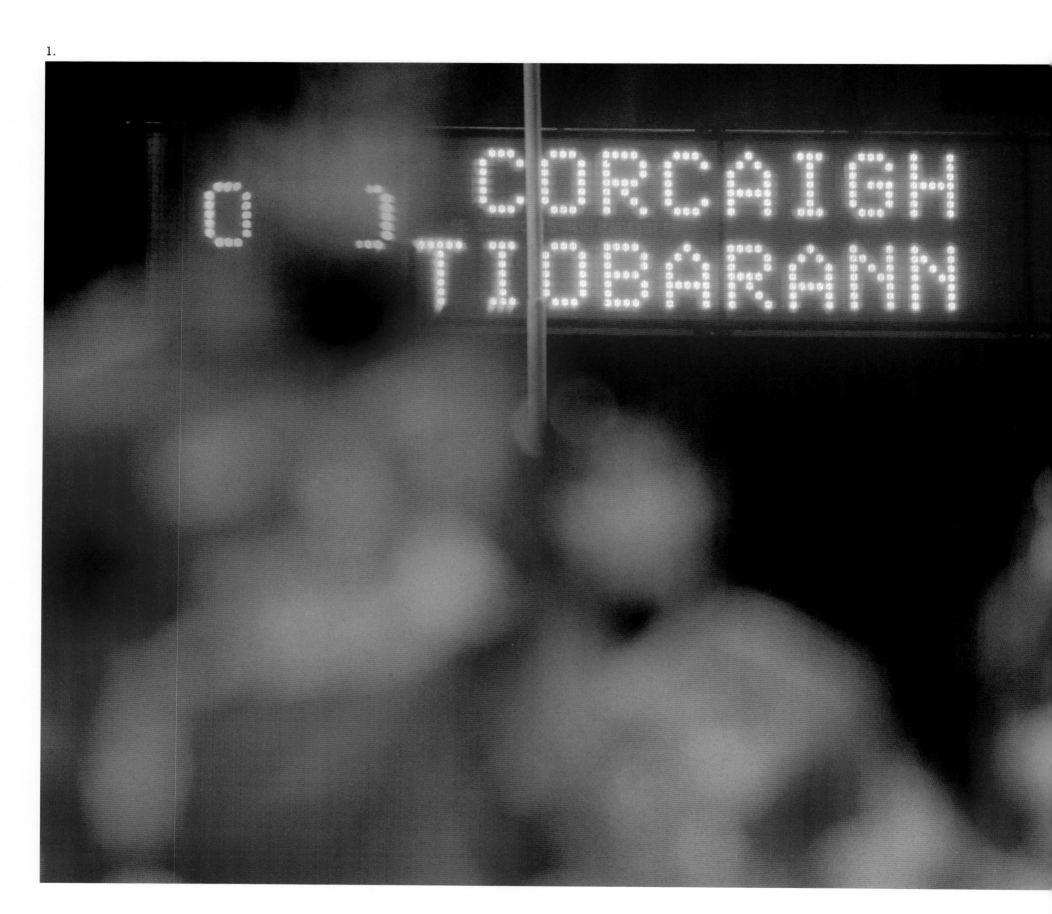

" I have said it before and I'll say it again, there are going to be good days and bad days, though it was nice to have the support today when our backs were to the wall **"**

Clare manager Davy Fitzgerald is happy after their league win over Galway in Ennis

5.

6.

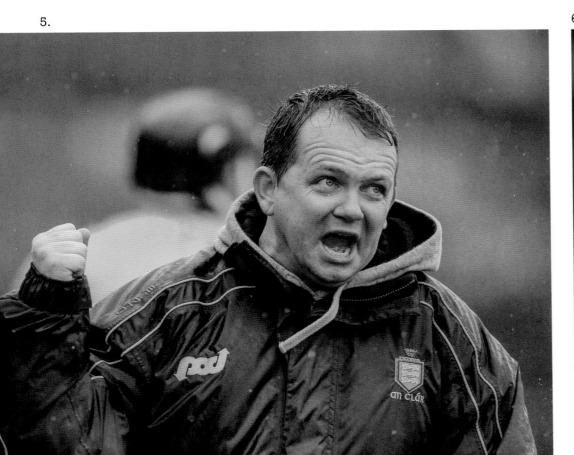

(1) Early wobble. The Wexford trio of Brian Malone, Shane Roche and Rory Quinlivan digest a nine-point reversal against Derry

(2) Two and one make three – yeah? An animated Kieran Donaghy makes his point to referee Eddie Kinsella in Kerry's league defeat to Kildare

(3) Collared. Mark Donnelly attempts to check the run of Rory Kavanagh as Tyrone edge out Donegal in a dress rehearsal for the counties' Ulster opener

(4) Frozen at Fraher Field. March is still with us and Shane Walsh adopts unorthodox methods to get the blood flowing as Waterford draw with Cork

(5) Wet, but temperature rising? Davy Fitzgerald acknowledges the final whistle, confirming a home win over Galway

(6) Deep in thought. Kilkenny manager Brian Cody takes stock during his team's Thurles defeat to Tipperary

10 Allianz GAA Football National League - Croke Park, Dublin
Kildare 2-07   Dublin 2-20

16 Allianz GAA Football National League - Páirc Uí Rinn, Cork
Cork 0-12   Donegal 0-10

1.

2.

(1) Wilting Lilies? Downbeat Kildare trudge off after a heavy beating at the hands of Dublin at Croke Park. Team manager Kieran McGeeney walks among the pack

(2) Seeing the light? Donegal manager Jim McGuinness is fully focused despite the distracting backdrop. Cork come out tops in this Leeside night-time assignment

1.

16 Allianz GAA Hurling National League - Páirc Uí Rinn, Cork
Cork 1-16 Clare 1-22

Allianz GAA Football National League - Croke Park, Dublin
Dublin 1-14 Tyrone 0-18

2.

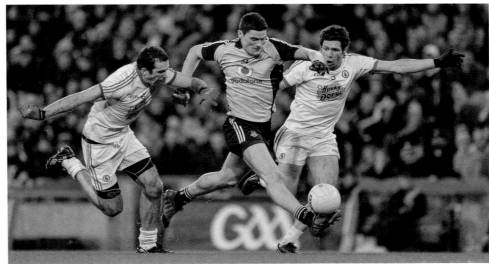

(1) Bullet the Blue Sky. Clare goalkeeper Patrick Kelly sticks to the confines of the small parallelogram before launching one under Páirc Uí Rinn's lights. It's a fixture that will pockmark the season. Advantage Clare here

(2) Poise and balance. Diarmuid Connolly soloes off the right with Justin McMahon and Seán Cavanagh in tow. It turns out to be Dublin's only competitive defeat of 2013

1.

24 Allianz GAA Hurling National League - Pearse Stadium, Salthill
Galway 2-12   Cork 2-12

Allianz GAA Football National League - Austin Stack Park, Tralee
Kerry 0-11   Cork 0-07

1.

2.

3.

(1) A trick shot. Galway manager Anthony Cunningham is not shaking hands with a three-handed man before his team's draw with Cork. Look closely and you will see that one man is photographing him and that the hand belongs to someone else

(2) A hop, skip and a jump. Six-year-old Kerry supporter Jack Mangan of Rylane, Co Cork makes his way down the Austin Stack Park steps before the hosts see off their old rivals

(3) The one that got away? Wayne McNamara's pose says it all after Limerick are pipped by Dublin in the Division One B play-off. Better days lie ahead… for both counties

APRIL '13

6   Allianz GAA Hurling National League Division 1B Final - Semple Stadium, Thurles
    Dublin 1-16   Limerick 1-15

    Allianz GAA Football National League - Athletic Grounds, Armagh
    Armagh 0-21   Galway 1-12

    Allianz GAA Football National League - Páirc Uí Chaoimh, Cork
    Cork 0-10   Mayo 0-11

4.

5.

" We are trying out different tactics at different stages. Whether you are missing players or not, you still have to try and play to different plans and try and adapt. We decided to go that way and will adapt as the year goes on **"**

Cork manager Conor Counihan explains the defensive tactics used by his under-strength team against Kerry in the league game at Tralee

(4) Way over the top? Gary O'Donnell opts for the unconventional, going up and over as Armagh's James Lavery hides the goods, with Paul Conroy on the bottom of the pile

(5) Crowded house. Aidan O'Shea makes a burst in an attempt to avoid traffic on a useful day for Mayo down by the Lee

14 Allianz GAA Football National League Semi-Final - Croke Park, Dublin
Tyrone 2-15   Kildare 2-11

Allianz GAA Hurling National League Division 2A Final - O'Connor Park, Tullamore
Laois 3-14   Westmeath 1-09

Allianz GAA Football National League Semi-Final - Croke Park, Dublin
Dublin 2-16   Mayo 0-16

Allianz GAA Hurling National League Division 2B Final - St Conleth's Park, Newbridge
London 1-16   Meath 1-14

1.

2.

❝ When people talk about the entry fee being worth it to see players, I don't think you will see better scores than the last two that Stephen O'Neill scored today. They were just something else ❞

Tyrone manager Mickey Harte praises Stephen O'Neill's sensational late points against Kildare

4.

(1) Coolness personified. Mattie Donnelly is calm and deliberate as he prepares to strike while Kildare's Niall Kelly shows more urgency. Tyrone prevail

(2) Satisfaction. Laois captain Matthew Whelan performs the honours after the O'Moore county see off Westmeath in the Division Two A hurling final

(3) A scene from 'Strictly'? Mayo's Colm Boyle gets all tangled with Kevin O'Brien as Michael Darragh Macauley seems to look the other way

(4) No holding back here. London hurling captain John Walsh lifts the trophy with unreserved joy after their Division Two B final success over Meath

14 Allianz GAA Hurling National League Division 3B Final - Páirc Seán Mac Diarmada, Carrick-on-Shannon
Longford 1-08   Sligo 0-09

Allianz GAA Hurling National League Division 1A Relegation Play-off - Gaelic Grounds, Limerick
Clare 0-31   Cork 2-23

1.

2.

(1) That winning feeling. Another win, another jubilant team shot. It's Longford's turn this time
after a Division Three B hurling final win over Sligo

(2) We start them young around here. Two-year-old Conor Riordan from Kilmallock, Co Limerick
tries out the photo bench for size before Clare's relegation play-off win over Cork

27 Allianz GAA Football National League Division 3 Final - Croke Park, Dublin
Monaghan 2-16   Meath 3-08

Allianz GAA Football National League Division 4 Final - Croke Park, Dublin
Limerick 0-16   Offaly 1-11

28 Allianz GAA Football National League Division 2 Final - Croke Park, Dublin
Derry 1-18   Westmeath 0-15

Allianz GAA Football National League Division 1 Final - Croke Park, Dublin
Dublin 0-18   Tyrone 0-17

2.

3.

4.

(1) A portent of things to come? Monaghan celebrate with captain Eoin Lennon gripping the Division Three football silverware after victory over Meath at Croke Park

(2 / 3) It must be league football finals weekend. Limerick's Seánie Buckley gets in on the act after his team's success over Offaly. Derry's Mark Lynch follows his lead the next day after their win over Westmeath

(4) A man of few words. Dublin captain Stephen Cluxton refers to his notes during his acceptance speech after the Division One league final. A stern Tyrone challenge has been overcome, and this is a duty Cluxton will oversee twice more

4 Cadbury GAA Football Under-21 All-Ireland Championship Final - Gaelic Grounds, Limerick
Galway 1-14 Cork 1-11

Allianz GAA Hurling National League Division 1 Final - Nowlan Park, Kilkenny
Kilkenny 2-17 Tipperary 0-20

5 Connacht GAA Football Senior Championship - Gaelic Park, New York
New York 0-07 Leitrim 4-19

❝ It's a pity playing a National League final in Nowlan Park that Brian was not able to attend because that's where he would just love to be. So it's great that we won today and that we will have him back shortly **❞**

Kilkenny selector Michael Dempsey pays tribute to missing manager Brian Cody after their league final win

1.

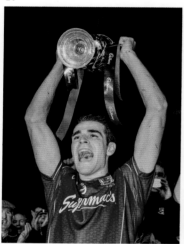

2.

3.

(1) Right man, right place. Galway under-21 football captain Fiontán Ó Curraoin crowns a day to remember by accepting All-Ireland silverware after he had given a midfield exhibition. Cork are the beaten finalists

(2) Normal service? For now at least. Kilkenny captain Colin Fennelly receives the league hurling final trophy after a Nowlan Park final win over Tipperary. Unusually this will be the last trophy lift for the team in 2013

(3) Bee swarm. Patrick Maher sets off, as only he does. Kieran Joyce, Tommy Walsh and JJ Delaney try to slow him up, as only they do

(4) It's a long way from Seán O'Heslins to here. Ballinamore man Pat Murray is greeted at Gaelic Park in the Bronx by Cork native Donie O'Sullivan before Leitrim's win over the Big Apple footballers

4.

18 Leinster GAA Hurling Senior Championship - Dr. Cullen Park, Carlow
Carlow 4-17 London 2-13

19 Leinster GAA Football Senior Championship - Cusack Park, Mullingar
Westmeath 3-15 Carlow 1-10

(1) Grip shortened, eyes fixed on the ball. London's John Walsh shapes to strike as Seán Murphy's hurley is sent out on blocking duty

(2) Triple-marked it matters not. Westmeath's Dessie Dolan gets his shot off despite the best efforts of Shane Mernagh, Barry John Molloy and Shane Redmond of Carlow. It's indicative of the edge held by Westmeath at home

❝ It was tight enough until Kieran Martin got the goal. I felt we lacked a bit of intensity in the second half, but I think there is more in us ❞

Westmeath manager Pat Flanagan after their easy win over Carlow in Mullingar

2.

19 Connacht GAA Football Senior Championship - Pearse Stadium, Salthill
Galway 0-11   Mayo 4-16

Ulster GAA Football Senior Championship - Kingspan Breffni Park, Cavan
Cavan 1-15   Armagh 1-11

25 Munster GAA Football Senior Championship - Gaelic Grounds, Limerick
Limerick 0-08   Cork 3-17

1.

" We were confident coming here today. We were favourites
coming into Galway's backyard and we knew that if we played
like we could, we were confident we could win **"**

**Mayo manager James Horan after their 17-point win over Galway at Salthill,
their biggest victory over Galway since 1907**

2.

(1) High fives. Mayo manager James Horan is given the pop star treatment before his team's run-out against Galway in Salthill. The optimism proves well founded

(2) The final nail in the coffin. Martin Dunne celebrates Cavan's last point in an eye-catching win over Armagh, as their Ulster campaign swings into life

(3) Keep me a seat. Cork football manager Conor Counihan takes in some of the intermediate game before the senior team's comfortable win over Limerick at the Gaelic Grounds

3.

26 Ulster GAA Football Senior Championship - MacCumhaill Park, Ballybofey
Donegal 2-10 Tyrone 0-10

Munster GAA Football Senior Championship - Fitzgerald Stadium, Killarney
Kerry 2-19 Tipperary 0-08

Leinster GAA Football Senior Championship - O'Moore Park, Portlaoise
Laois 1-06 Louth 1-16

1.

2.

" Tyrone really had us in their sights, so winning in those circumstances is the most satisfying thing for us **"**

Donegal manager Jim McGuinness after the reigning All-Ireland champions open their title defence with victory over Tyrone in Ballybofey

4.

(1) A Donegal wrap? It's mixed allegiances for the providers of culinary refreshments at MacCumhaill Park as Kathleen Martin from Ballybofey and Aishling Kelly from Letterkenny flank Elaine McDonald of Cookstown

(2) Pretty in pink… gloves. Colm McFadden celebrates a goal in Donegal's Ulster championship home win over Tyrone and the defending All-Ireland champions' campaign is up and running

(3) He who leaps highest. Johnny Buckley of Kerry does battle with Robbie Costigan in what turns out to be a one-sided win for the Kingdom over Tipperary

(4) They have soldiered together but not today. Laois manager Justin McNulty congratulates his former Armagh team-mate Aidan O'Rourke after Louth's championship win in Portlaoise

26 Leinster GAA Football Senior Championship - County Grounds, Aughrim
Wicklow 1-15   Longford 0-16

Connacht GAA Football Senior Championship - Emerald Park, Ruislip
London 1-12   Sligo 0-14

(1) Not much leg room on this flight. Longford's Damien Sheridan dives full length, ball in hand, to fend off Seánie Furlong, left, and Austin O'Malley of Wicklow

(2) It was a while coming. Ciarán McCallion's no-holds-barred celebration reminds us how long London have waited for a Connacht championship win. Previous Connacht and qualifier performances hinted that this was coming, and Sligo are the victims

1.

2.

3.

9 Leinster GAA Football Senior Championship - County Grounds, Drogheda
Louth 1-15 Wexford 2-13

Munster GAA Hurling Senior Championship - Gaelic Grounds, Limerick
Limerick 1-18 Tipperary 1-15

❝ We played with a huge intensity last year as well, but when it came to the last 10 minutes we didn't have the quality of player coming in that they had, whereas this year we did **❞**

Limerick hurling manager John Allen pays tribute to his substitutes after their shock win over Tipperary in the Munster championship at the Gaelic Grounds

1.   2.

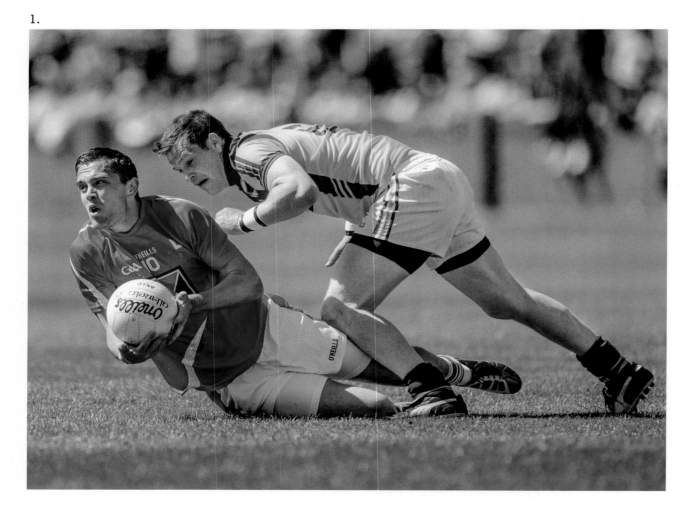

(1) The rule book says 'clear striking action'. Louth's Andy McDonnell offloads despite an entanglement with David Murphy of Wexford. Louth don't build on their impressive opening-round win over Laois

(2) The sliotar, the strike, the hook. Classic Munster hurling as Limerick's Graeme Mulcahy swings to strike and Michael Cahill tries to hook him. Limerick lay down a marker

15 Leinster GAA Hurling Senior Championship Replay - Parnell Park, Dublin
Dublin 1-17   Wexford 0-12

Leinster GAA Football Senior Championship - County Grounds, Aughrim
Wicklow 1-12   Meath 1-17

16 Ulster GAA Football Senior Championship - Brewster Park, Enniskillen
Fermanagh 0-11   Cavan 0-13

Connacht GAA Football Senior Championship - Elverys MacHale Park, Castlebar
Mayo 0-21   Roscommon 0-09

2.

3.

4.

(1) Swinging in the rain. An early sunshower in no way distracts the 12 players scrambling for possession in the early stages of Dublin's replay with Wexford. Despite a feisty start, the Dubs pull away in the end

(2) Gone for another year. Wicklow are the only county never to win the Leinster title, and Damian Power contemplates the completion of another barren provincial campaign after defeat to Meath

(3) Dunne deal. A familiar sight from the opening stages of the championship as Martin Dunne asks questions of John Woods and the Fermanagh rearguard

(4) Man, ball, the lot. Alan Freeman of Mayo challenges Neil Collins and goalkeeper Darren O'Malley of Roscommon in the counties' Connacht semi-final. Mayo's challenge gathers more momentum

16 Ulster GAA Hurling Senior Championship - Páirc Esler, Newry
Down 3-20   Armagh 1-11

Munster GAA Football Senior Championship - Cusack Park, Ennis
Clare 1-11   Cork 1-20

Leinster GAA Hurling Senior Championship - O'Moore Park, Portlaoise
Laois 1-13   Galway 2-17

1.

2

3.

(1) Ball to hand? Declan Coulter of Armagh waits for the sliotar to drop as Conor Woods closes in. Down make progress on the Ulster circuit

(2) We train as hard as they do but... Captain Gary Brennan and his Clare team-mates are game against Cork but the gap cannot be bridged on this day

(3) What might have been. Laois manager Séamus Plunkett is lost in thought towards the end of his team's defeat to Galway, though the margin does his team no justice

22   GAA Hurling All-Ireland Senior Championship Preliminary Round - Wexford Park, Wexford
Wexford 3-18   Antrim 0-17

GAA Hurling All-Ireland Senior Championship Preliminary Round - Emerald Park, Ruislip
London 0-11   Westmeath 1-15

GAA Hurling All-Ireland Senior Championship Preliminary Round - O'Connor Park, Tullamore
Offaly 1-14   Waterford 0-21

1.

2.

(1) No quarter asked or given. Wexford's Paul Morris, his face obscured, does what has to be done to halt the march of Antrim's Odhran McFadden down by the Slaney. Antrim's interest in the Liam MacCarthy Cup ends

(2) As the great 'P Sé' might have said - 'at your dead ease'. Six London-based exiles, Mick Colgan from Westmeath, Mick Kirwan from Cork, Kilkennyman Tony McBride, Johnny Hoare from Kildare, Tipperary man Pat Ely and John Twomey from Cork, make themselves comfortable at Ruislip for the visit of Westmeath

(3) Sincerity. Waterford manager Michael Ryan is grateful to leave Tullamore with a win over Offaly and doesn't mind telling his opposite number Ollie Baker, whose tenure will end with this reversal

30 Connacht GAA Football Senior Championship Replay - Dr Hyde Park, Roscommon
London 2-11   Leitrim 1-13

Ulster GAA Football Senior Championship - Croke Park, Dublin
Dublin 4-16   Kildare 1-09

GAA Football All-Ireland Senior Championship Round 1 - Owenbeg, Derry
Derry 0-15   Sligo 0-08

1.

“ It has taken us three years to build this team, but it goes back much longer than that. Getting to a Connacht final is a reward for all the people who put the work in down through the years in London ”
London manager Paul Coggins after their Connacht semi-final win over Leitrim at Dr Hyde Park

1.

2.

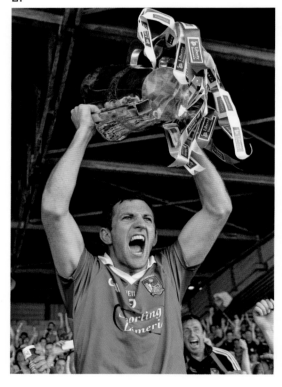

" It's a great achievement and is just reward for a team that has been very honest in everything they have done on and off the field **"**

Limerick manager John Allen pays tribute to his team after their Munster hurling final win over Cork, their first title since 1996

14 Munster GAA Hurling Senior Championship Final - Gaelic Grounds, Limerick
Limerick 0-24   Cork 0-15

(1) Hand-eye co-ordination. Graeme Mulcahy and Conor O'Sullivan reach for the sliotar with the Cork man grabbing it

(2) Who said provincial titles don't matter anymore? Limerick captain Donal O'Grady's delight provides an insight into the significance of the win

(3) Silverware safely ensconced. The sanctuary of a winning dressingroom is truly something to behold, as any player who has played at any level will testify

(Overleaf) A sea of green. Limerick supporters invade the sward in anticipation of the trophy lift and speeches. It was never going to be any other way if they won

3.

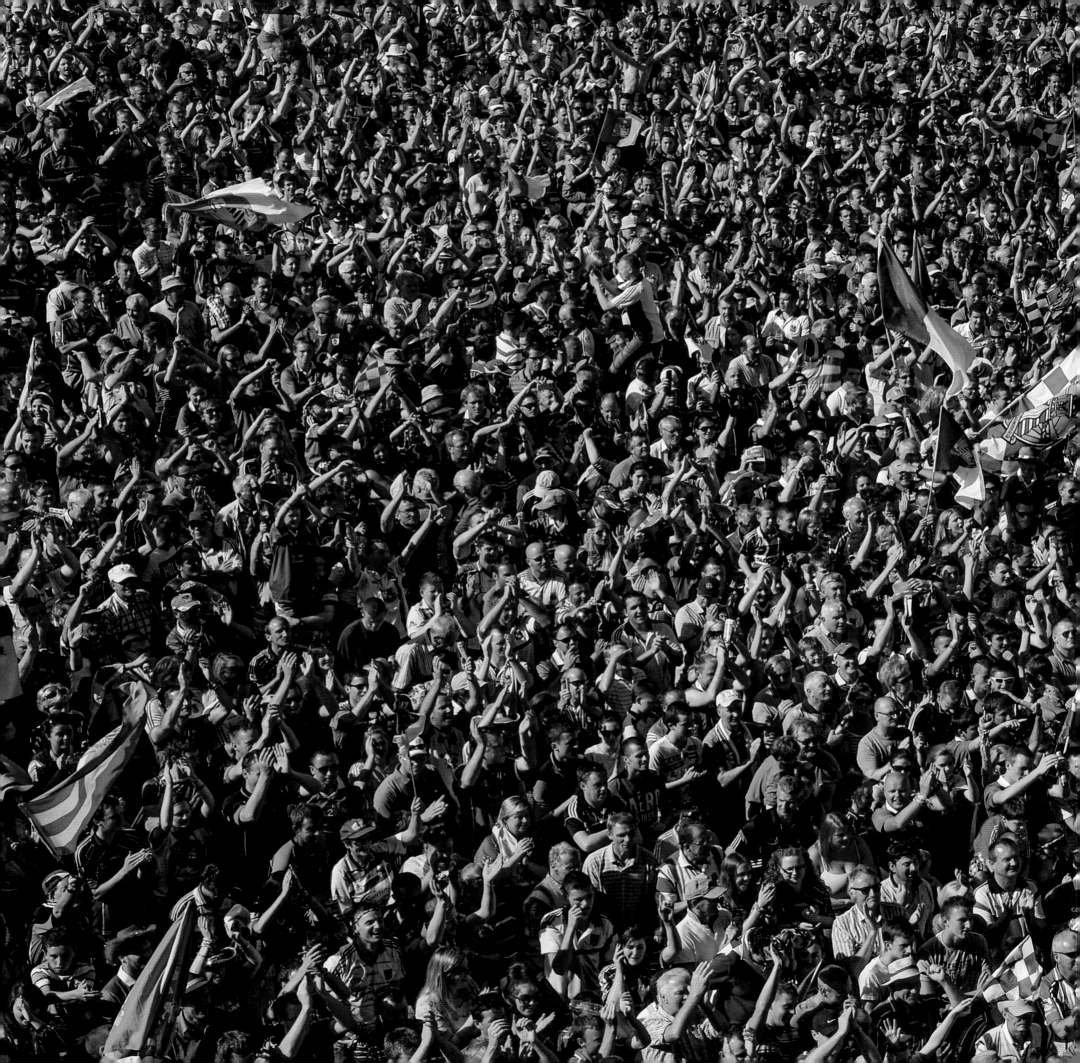

20 GAA Football All-Ireland Senior Championship Round 3 - Wexford Park, Wexford
Wexford 2-08   Laois 0-16

GAA Football All-Ireland Senior Championship Round 3 - Celtic Park, Derry
Derry 0-20   Cavan 1-22

GAA Football All-Ireland Senior Championship Round 3 - St Conleth's Park, Newbridge
Kildare 0-12   Tyrone 1-11

GAA Football All-Ireland Senior Championship Round 3 - Pearse Stadium, Salthill
Galway 1-11   Armagh 0-09

1.

2.

(1) Brothers in arms. Laois players link for the playing of Amhrán na bhFiann at Wexford. A similar unity of purpose gets them through

(2) Holding on. Eugene Keating gets away from Patsy Bradley with arms as opposed to hand. Cavan's bright season continues on away soil

(3) Sunday best on a Saturday. The regulation white jacket can be ditched on a glorious night in Newbridge. Tyrone trouble the umpires more than Kildare and for the right reasons too

(4) Did that just happen? Armagh manager Paul Grimley grips his knees while trying to decipher what he has just seen

3 GAA Football All-Ireland Senior Championship Quarter-Final - Croke Park, Dublin
Tyrone 0-14   Monaghan 0-12

GAA Football All-Ireland Senior Championship Quarter-Final - Croke Park, Dublin
Dublin 1-16   Cork 0-14

1.

(1) Blindsided? Monaghan's eventual All-Star nominee goalkeeper Rory Beggan bears the brunt and dunt of Aidan Cassidy's tackle. Tyrone's guile and experience see them home at Croke Park

(2) The top corner is calling. Jack McCaffrey's clipped effort beats Alan Quirke, who does everything asked of a goalkeeper, making himself big and staying up until the last minute. Neither Quirke nor Thomas Clancy can deny Dublin their win

2.

" What pleased me most was the great character among the group. They showed great energy, great steadfastness and a willingness never to give up. They could have got frustrated by some of the goal opportunities that they created without taking, but they kept at it **"**

Dublin manager Jim Gavin after the All-Ireland quarter-final win over Cork

4 GAA Football All-Ireland Senior Championship Quarter-Final - Croke Park, Dublin
   Kerry 0-15 Cavan 0-09

GAA Football All-Ireland Senior Championship Quarter-Final - Croke Park, Dublin
Mayo 4-17 Donegal 1-10

(1) Swan Lake? Cavan's Cian Mackey goes full stretch but the leather is already
safely in the hands of Peter Crowley of Kerry. Split seconds and all that. Kerry
do enough to book a semi-final ticket

(2) Coming down but to whom? Mayo midfielder Séamus O'Shea reaches for the
high ball with Donegal's Michael Murphy and Neil Gallagher as O'Shea's team-
mates, the half-back line of Donal Vaughan, Lee Keegan and Colm Boyle, are on
standby. Mayo don't lose many contests in this game

1.

2.

11   GAA Hurling All-Ireland Senior Championship Semi-Final - Croke Park, Dublin
Cork 1-24   Dublin 1-19

18   GAA Hurling All-Ireland Senior Championship Semi-Final - Croke Park, Dublin
Clare 1-22   Limerick 0-18

1.

2.

" It was the first time I saw a Cork team celebrate after a semi-final win, but they were entitled to it by their application and work rate from start to finish "

Former Cork manager Donal O'Grady after his county's win over Dublin

4.

(1) The clincher. GAA goals are not always lustily celebrated but this one is – and deservedly so. Patrick Horgan strikes late to break Dublin hearts and crown Cork's passage to the final

(2) Two loyal Cork servants. Between them they have seen it all before but there is something about semi-final successes. Cork manager Jimmy Barry Murphy and county secretary Frank Murphy share a special moment

(3) A very local affair. Clare and Limerick decamp to the capital for the second hurling semi-final. Limerick's Richie McCarthy adjusts his leap in mid-flow while Cathal McInerney opts for the stick

(4) Clare jig. Cathal McInerney celebrates at the final whistle

2.

❝ Today was a grind, the hardest game we had, certainly in the first half. We were playing poor stuff, but we kept going and battling ❞

Mayo manager James Horan on his team's hard-fought semi-final win

(1) The shoulder-tackle of the year? Gaelic football at this level is no longer played by small, light men – or at least by very few. Tom Cunniffe clatters into Peter Harte and Harte leaves the field soon after. It's the end for Tyrone also

(2) 'You'll be back'. Alan Freeman, in the Tyrone colours, commiserates with Conor Gormley after Mayo's success

1.

(1)   Frozen I. Donnchadh Walsh is still captured in striking pose despite the journey of the ball to the Hill 16 net. The pass from Colm Cooper to set up this scoring chance is not bettered all season

(2)   Frozen II. Point or goal effort, it matters not. What have Kerry done to Kevin McManamon? The St Jude's clubman lifts the ball over Brendan Kealy after a trademark goalward shuffle and the game tilts towards the blue camp

❝ I thought a defender was going to come to me but they kind of played half between myself and the two boys on the wing. So I said I would try to aim for the crossbar and it might squeeze under it or it will go over and we might get something out of it ❞

Kevin McManamon on the late goal he scored to break Kerry hearts in a magnificent All-Ireland semi-final at Croke Park

" It's what you dream of as young fella. You think that it's a dream, you never think that it is actually going to happen **"**

Waterford captain Kevin Daly after their win over Galway in the All-Ireland minor hurling final, the Déise's first success at this level since 1948

1.

3.

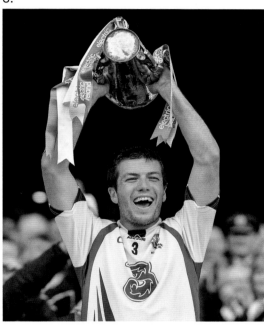

(1) Minor miracle. Waterford's first All-Ireland minor hurling title since 1948 and Patrick Curran savours the moment after scoring their first goal

(2) Running and jumping for joy. Waterford's Michael Kearney, Austin Gleeson, Micheál Harney and Stephen Bennett pull the celebration cord after their All-Ireland minor success

(3) The smile says it all. Waterford minor captain Kevin Daly lifts the Irish Press Cup after their win over Galway

Let's all do the Klinsmann. It's doubtful whether one of Germany's finest has heard
of Croke Park, never mind the Waterford hurlers' minor success, but they've
heard of him. Captain Kevin Daly leads the way

8 GAA Hurling All-Ireland Senior Championship Final - Croke Park, Dublin
Clare 0-25   Cork 3-16

1.

(1) Army inspection? Like a general, Davy Fitzgerald appears to be eyeballing his Clare troops before sending them into battle

(2) Nails, what nails? The buzz word is tentative for JBM as he surveys what's unfolding before him. With good reason at times too

❝ There are a lot of places we need to improve, the players know that themselves. I thought a draw was a fair result **❞**

Cork manager Jimmy Barry Murphy after the drawn All-Ireland hurling final against Clare

1.

8 GAA Hurling All-Ireland Senior Championship Final - Croke Park, Dublin
Clare 0-25   Cork 3-16

2.

3.

(1) Anthony Nash lifts, Nash somehow encroaches, Nash strikes, Nash scores. Cork's goalkeeper unleashes a rocket and Clare's team of five in the small parallelogram are rendered redundant

(2) Cometh the hour and all that. Domhnall O'Donovan picks the best time imaginable to score his first competitive point in intercounty hurling. Stephen White and Cork were only seconds away from victory. The final finishes level for the second time in 12 months and only the second time since 1959

(3) No presentation today but do join us in 13 days' time for the first floodlit All-Ireland final. Croke Park steward Colm Smith is the unexpected recipient of the Liam MacCarthy Cup at full time

14 Bord Gáis Energy GAA Hurling Under-21 All-Ireland Championship Final - Semple Stadium, Thurles
Clare 2-28   Antrim 0-12

15 Liberty Insurance All-Ireland Senior Camogie Championship Final - Croke Park, Dublin
Galway 1-09   Kilkenny 0-07

1.

2.

3.

4.

(1) No stopping Clare. Shane O'Donnell finds top stride as Antrim's Matthew Donnelly attempts to halt his gallop and a good year for the Banner gets considerably better with the All-Ireland under-21 title on the sideboard

(2) It's good to talk. Or listen. Davy Fitzgerald takes his seat for the under-21 hurling final – a welcome distraction between All-Ireland final assignments

(3) Follow our lead. Clare captain Paul Flanagan lifts the under-21 hurling trophy and throws down the gauntlet to the seniors

(4) On a Clare day. A snapshot of an idyllic afternoon for Clare hurling as Semple Stadium is theirs – albeit temporarily – at the end of the under-21 hurling final

(5) Getting away. Galway's Noreen Coen attempts to rise the sliotar as Kilkenny's Edwina Keane loses her footing. The ladies in maroon finish in front

(6) Presidential seals of approval. The President of Ireland, Michael D Higgins, applauds as the president of the Camogie Association, Aileen Lawlor, presents Lorraine Ryan with the cup

1.

2.

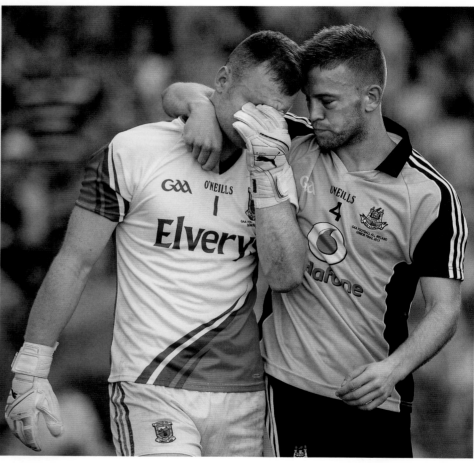

3.

" We are devastated. There were tears there in the dressingroom. But we are going to keep fighting and we will be back. We are a very good team. The only problem was Donegal were a very good team and played better on the day and Dublin are a very good team and played very well today and took their chances "

Mayo captain Andy Moran after the Connacht champions had lost another All-Ireland final, this time to Dublin

(1) Pitch black on glorious technicolour. The unmistakable outline of James Horan contrasts with a sun-drenched Hill 16

(2) College colleagues. The jersey colour may differ today but respect runs deep between former DCU team-mates Jonny Cooper of Dublin and Mayo goalkeeper Rob Hennelly

(3) Confined joy from the captain. A deadpan Stephen Cluxton raises Sam skyward - cue the sky-blue raptures

(4) The ultimate satisfaction? It's delivering when it matters most. The season may have been a slow burner for Bernard Brogan but ask Kerry and Mayo about the influence of the Dublin forward when the chips are down

2.

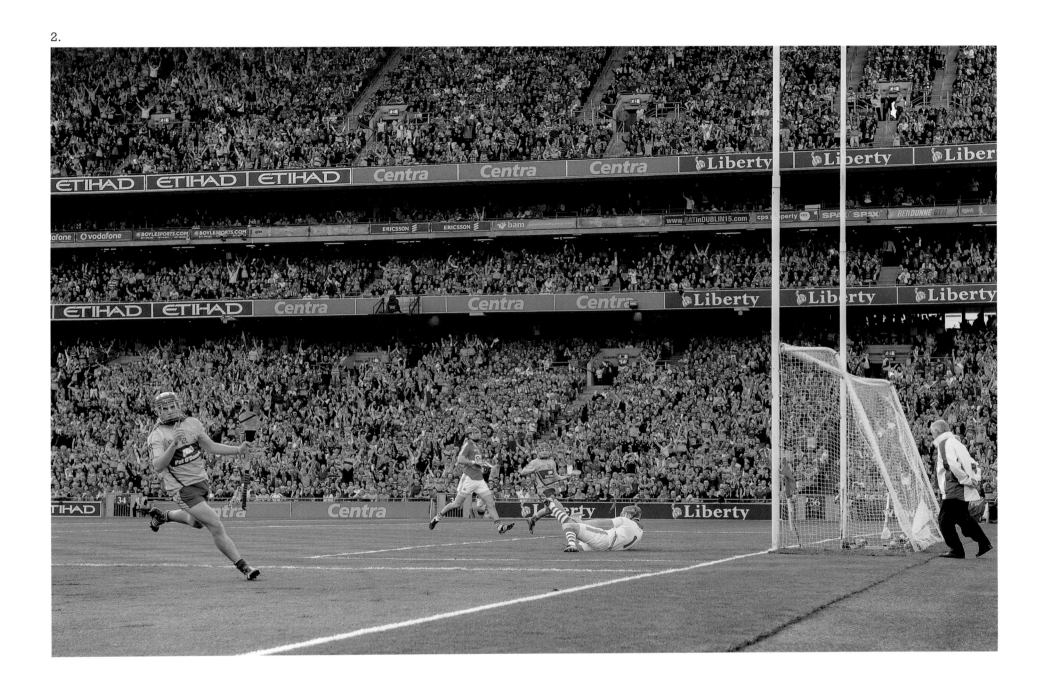

(1) Lights, camera and a classic. The Croke Park lights are used from the word go for the hurling replay and the quality of what follows ensures that a talking point before the game is quickly forgotten about

(2) Shane O'Who? A surprise selection for the replay, Clare corner forward Shane O'Donnell has notched the first score on his way to Banner County immortality. With Anthony Nash grounded and the sliotar nestling in the net he wheels away in acknowledgement of his feat

1.

2.

3.   4.

(1) Bodies on the line. Twelve Clare players take up positions in front of their net in an effort to deny Anthony Nash another goal. It seemed like a good idea but it's ultimately futile

(2) Almost Shefflinesque. Shane O'Donnell shortens the grip and bats home to avoid being hooked. It's a split-second decision of class that yields his and Clare's third goal, and leaves Cork with a mountain to climb

(3) Delicate touch. Colin Ryan seems to caress the sliotar with his hurley as he and Tom Kenny go full stretch

(4) Living every puck. An animated Davy Fitzgerald goes all Latino with his hand gestures on the most Irish of days in an effort to get his point across

3.

1.

2.

(1) That winning feeling. Conor McGrath has just dispatched a rocket at the Davin End goal and he knows that, as well as raising a green flag, he has put his team right back in the driving seat

(2) Needs must. Conor O'Sullivan prepares to lunge at the sliotar as Conor McGrath displays his ground skills

(3) Anything that lad O'Donnell can do... substitute Darach Honan improvises to force home his team's fifth goal to seal the deal

(4) If you could bottle this feeling. Pádraic Collins and Colm Galvin lead the celebrations as from virtually nowhere Clare's incredible season – and that of hurling as a whole - reaches its zenith. Few could claim they saw it coming

4

" The players have exceeded my expectations. My job is to take as much pressure off them as I can. In my heart of hearts I know anything is possible and to be honest I believe in them **"**

Clare manager Davy Fitzgerald gives credit to his players after winning the All-Ireland hurling title

1.

2.

3

" It's not a cliché, but the players were fantastic for us both days, showed tremendous spirit, showed fabulous pride in Cork hurling. We will take our defeat like men and move on "

Cork's Jimmy Barry Murphy praises his players despite the disappointment of their defeat to Clare

(1) Crouching tiger. Davy Fitzgerald contemplates the enormity of it all

(2) For every winner… Christopher Joyce can't hide the desolation at the final whistle. Some players never get here, others spend their careers trying to get back

(3) On the podium, in the pantheon. Clare captain Patrick Donnellan joins the list of Clare greats as only the fourth man to oversee the honour

(4) No time for slacking. With the ladies football finals to come the following day, the post-match stadium clean-up doesn't take long to swing into action

1.

2.

3.

(1) Go team. Monaghan form a huddle before the throw-in against Cork as the final words of encouragement and reminders of the game plan are aired

(2) Striking action. Valerie Mulcahy is a picture of concentration as she shoots to score Cork's goal despite the encroaching Sharon Courtney of Monaghan

(3) Yards separate them but they're worlds apart at this moment. Juliet Murphy of Cork is congratulated by the team masseuse Eleanor Lucey while Monaghan's Cathríona McConnell is forlorn on the ground

(4) Who says the enjoyment wanes in domination? Ann Marie Walsh delights in the moment of receiving the Brendan Martin Cup - Cork's eighth title in nine years

 Coming back here year after year is no sacrifice. There are people in hospitals who would love to be here "

Cork manager Eamonn Ryan in reflective mood after the Cork ladies beat Monaghan by one point to win their eighth All-Ireland title in nine years

OCTOBER '13

19 Irish Daily Mail International Rules Series - Kingspan Breffni Park, Cavan
Ireland 2-12-9 (57)   Australia 1-7-8 (35)

26 Irish Daily Mail International Rules Series - Croke Park, Dublin
Ireland 6-22-14 (116)   Australia 2-7-4 (37)

1.

2.

3.

" I don't see the problem in two players going at it, toe-to-toe, and having a bit of push and shove. That's all part of this game. And it should be. And it gets the crowd going. People see the passion and they get involved in that as well. So I think that needs to be brought back in "

Laois player Colm Begley arguing that the lack of full and proper physicality is hindering the International Rules series

4.

(1) Green giants. A competitive International Rules Test goes to Ulster for the first time when Ireland host Australia at Kingspan Breffni Park. Ireland are not found wanting on any front and their focus is evident during Amhrán na bhFiann

(2) Laois men reunited in green. They ply their trades in different codes and countries but Ross Munnelly is the first man to congratulate AFL-based Zach Tuohy after he scores Ireland's first goal

(3) He who leaps highest. Referee Matt Stevic remains grounded as Ireland's Colm Begley and Josh Hill of Australia contest a throw-in after Ireland's third goal. The pitch markings at Croke Park confirm this is not football as we know it

(4) Advance Ireland Fair. The retention of the Cormac McAnallen Cup confirmed following their second win, the victorious Irish players and backroom team celebrate a record Test and series success over Australia

GALLERY OF FANS

AWARD WINNING IMAGES
sportsfile

Relive all the agony and ecstasy of past campaigns

1997   1998   1999   2000   2001

2002   2003   2004   2005   2006

2007   2008   2009   2010   2011

2012

A limited number of back issues of *A Season of Sundays* are available for €29.95 each, including post and packaging.
To complete your set please send remittance, indicating the book(s) required, together with your name and address to:
Sportsfile, Patterson House, 14 South Circular Road, Portobello, Dublin 8, Ireland

Alternatively shop online at: **www.sportsfile.com**